D1162352

POETRY BASICS

○

NURSERY RHYMES

○

VALERIE BODDEN

CREATIVE ◖ EDUCATION

AC Cashiers Comm. Library
P.O. Box 2127
Cashiers NC 28717

Published by Creative Education
P.O. Box 227, Mankato, Minnesota 56002
Creative Education is an imprint of The Creative Company
www.thecreativecompany.us

Design and production by Stephanie Blumenthal
Printed by Corporate Graphics in the United States of America

Photographs by Alamy (Antiques & Collectables, Classic Image, Mary Evans Picture Library, Hilary
Morgan), American Antiquarian Society, The Bridgeman Art Library (Linda Edgerton, Paula Rego, John
Arthur Thompson, Fritz von Uhde), Corbis (Bettmann, Blue Lantern Studio, Michael Nicholson), Dreamstime
(Kcdesigns, Pusicmario), Getty Images (Dorling Kindersley), The Granger Collection, New York

Copyright © 2010 Creative Education
International copyright reserved in all countries.
No part of this book may be reproduced in any form
without written permission from the publisher.

Library of Congress Cataloging-in-Publication Data
Bodden, Valerie.
Nursery rhymes / by Valerie Bodden.
p. cm. — (Poetry basics)
Includes bibliographical references and index.
ISBN 978-1-58341-778-2
1. Nursery rhymes, English—History and criticism—Juvenile literature.
2. Nursery rhymes, American—History and criticism—Juvenile literature.
3. Nursery rhymes—History and criticism—Juvenile literature. I. Title. II. Series.

PR976.B63 2009
398.8'0941—dc22   2008009157

CPSIA: 021612 PO1551
4 6 8 9 7 5

People have written poems for thousands of years. Long ago, when people wanted to tell a story, they made it into a poem. Today, people write poems about all kinds of topics, from sunsets to traffic jams. Poems can help readers see things in a new way. They can make readers laugh or cry, sigh or scream. The goal of the short, often silly poems known as nursery rhymes usually is to entertain and soothe babies and young children.

RHYMES THROUGH TIME

No one knows exactly how long children have been entertained by nursery rhymes. There is evidence that up to 2,000 years ago, nursery tales and songs somewhat similar to today's nursery rhymes (although they didn't necessarily rhyme) were being told in nurseries throughout Europe.

The earliest of the nursery rhymes still known today are believed to have been created before the 1600s. And at least half of all nursery rhymes are probably more than 200 years old. Similar versions of many of these old rhymes, such as "Humpty Dumpty," existed in countries across Europe.

The first nursery rhymes were not written down. They were passed on **orally**. Many of the rhymes were not even originally created for children. Some were parts of songs meant for adults. Others were taken from the cries of **vendors** in the streets. Some were parts of old religious traditions.

Over time, these rhymes became part of children's daily lives. But it wasn't until the beginning of the 1700s that a few of the rhymes were finally published in England as *A Little Book for Little Children*. Then, around 1744, *Tommy Thumb's Pretty Song Book* was printed in England. The tiny book contained a number of nursery rhymes that are still well known today. For example, the book's version of "Baa, Baa, Black Sheep"(as shown on the next page) is nearly the same as the version many people know today.

Bah, Bah, a black Sheep,
Have you any Wool,
Yes merry have I,
Three Bags full,
One for my Master,
One for my Dame,
One for my Little Boy
That lives in the lane.

Sometime between 1765 and 1780, a collection of rhymes called *Mother Goose's Melody* was published in England by John Newbery. The book became an instant success, and copies were soon being sold throughout England and in America. The book was so popular that the name "Mother Goose" soon came to describe all traditional nursery rhymes in America.

Although many of the most popular nursery rhymes already existed by the late 1700s, rhymes continued to be written after the publication of *Mother Goose's Melody*. In 1830, American writer Sarah Josepha Hale penned the words of what has become one of the best-known rhymes in the English language: "Mary Had a Little Lamb."

Mary had a little lamb,
    Its fleece was white as snow;
And everywhere that Mary went
    The lamb was sure to go.

Although the writing of new nursery rhymes is not common today, the old favorites continue to be recited again and again by children around the world. These little poems are still part of many people's earliest—and often happiest—memories.

MUSICAL AND MEMORABLE

There are so many different types of nursery rhymes that there is no specific form that this kind of poetry can take. Some nursery rhymes are short, with four or fewer lines. Others are long and contain many verses.

Almost all nursery rhymes are musical. This doesn't mean that all nursery rhymes are songs (although many can be sung). It means that most nursery rhymes have a very strong feeling of rhyme and **rhythm**. And their rhyme and rhythm make nursery rhymes easy to remember.

Little Miss Muffet, she sat on a tuffet
Eating of curds and whey;
There came a little Spider, and sat down beside her,
and frighted Miss Muffet away

Words that rhyme end in the same sound. For example, "hello" rhymes with "yellow," and "red" rhymes with "dead." (Notice that words do not have to be spelled the same way to rhyme.) Although most nursery rhymes use the technique of rhyming, a nursery rhyme does not have to follow a specific **rhyme scheme**.

Some nursery rhymes follow the rhyme scheme *aabb*. The letter *a* stands for the first rhyming sound. So the last sounds of lines one and two rhyme with each other. The letter *b* stands for the second rhyming sound. Lines three and four end with this sound. The following nursery rhyme uses this rhyme scheme. (In the rhyme, the word "petticoat" means a type of clothing worn under a skirt.)

Little Nancy Etticoat
With a white petticoat,
And a red nose,
The longer she stands the shorter she grows.

"PAT-A-CAKE PAT-A-CAKE"

Notice in the nursery rhyme that new words such as "Etticoat" can even be made up to make the lines of the poem rhyme! The *aabb* rhyme scheme is one of many that can be used in nursery rhymes. Other rhyme schemes might consist of *abab* or *aabcc* patterns.

Along with their fun rhymes, nursery rhymes also usually have a strong sense of rhythm. The rhythm of a poem is like the beat of a drum. It keeps the poem moving forward. When we speak, we say some words or parts of words with more **stress** than others. A nursery rhyme's combination of stressed and unstressed **syllables** helps make up its rhythm. In the nursery rhyme on the next page, the stressed syllables are in capital letters.

HUMPty DUMPty SAT on a WALL,
HUMPty DUMPty HAD a great FALL.
  ALL the king's HORSes,
  And ALL the king's MEN,
COULDn't put HUMPty toGETher aGAIN.

As with rhyme scheme, nursery rhymes do not have to follow a specific rhythm. Reading a nursery rhyme out loud can help you to identify its rhythm. In fact, since nursery rhymes were originally passed on orally, they are usually meant to be heard rather than simply seen on a page.

NONSENSE AND VIOLENCE

J ust as nursery rhymes follow a number of different forms, they are also about a number of different subjects. Nursery rhymes have been written about everything from people and animals to the weather and **superstitions**. They cover a wide range of emotions, too, including joy, sadness, fear, and love. But no matter how serious their subject matter, most nursery rhymes are lighthearted.

Some nursery rhymes tell stories about real people. Others are about made-up characters. Because the history behind many nursery rhymes has been lost, it's sometimes hard to figure out which characters were real and which were made up. Some people believe that the nursery rhymes about Old King Cole and Little Miss Muffet may have been based on real people. Old Mother Hubbard is probably a made-up nursery rhyme character.

Although some nursery rhymes are about things that actually did or could happen, others are complete **nonsense**. Some nonsense rhymes consist of made-up words. Others contain ridiculous or impossible situations. The following nursery rhyme contains both nonsense words and a nonsense situation.

Hey diddle diddle,

The cat and the fiddle,

The cow jumped over the moon;

The little dog laughed

To see such sport,

And the dish ran away with the spoon.

While nonsense verses are usually seen as a source of fun for children, people at various times have called some nursery rhymes "inappropriate" for children. Because many nursery rhymes were not originally intended for children, some contained references to rude jokes, drinking, or death. From the 1500s through the 1700s, most people did not see this as a problem, since children were often looked on as "mini-adults." But during the mid- to late 1800s, that view changed, and a number of nursery rhymes were rewritten to make them more suitable for children.

Even with these changes, many nursery rhymes are still fairly violent in nature. Some refer to murder, death, cruelty, stealing, dishonesty, or kidnapping. For example, "Three Blind Mice" seems to suggest an attitude of cruelty toward animals.

Three blind mice, three blind mice,
See how they run, see how they run,
They all ran after the farmer's wife,
She cut off their tails with a carving knife,
Did you ever see such a sight in your life,
    As three blind mice?

Yet most people today believe that even the most violent nursery rhymes are no cause for concern, since children know that the rhymes are not real. Some people even think that it's good for nursery rhymes to cover such topics. After all, they argue, children have to deal with death and other difficult subjects in the real world.

KINDS OF RHYMES

The title "nursery rhyme" has been given to a wide variety of children's poems. Among the first types of nursery rhymes were probably "infant amusements." These are games meant to entertain babies. "Pat-a-cake" is one of the early infant amusements still enjoyed by babies today.

Riddles were also among early nursery rhymes. A riddle is a word puzzle. It contains clues to help readers figure out the answer to the puzzle. For example, "Little Nancy Etticoat" on page 12 is a riddle. Look at that rhyme again. Can you figure out who—or what—Little Nancy Etticoat is? (Hint: It is something that gives off light—and sometimes a pleasant scent.)

Another type of rhyme that could be heard in the nursery early on was the lullaby. Although lullabies were meant to calm infants, their words weren't always soothing. For example, if you look closely at "Rock-a-Bye Baby," you'll see that if babies understood the words, they might be frightened rather than comforted.

Rock-a-bye baby, in the treetop,

When the wind blows, the cradle will rock;

When the bough breaks, the cradle will fall,

Down will come baby, cradle and all.

A B C D

Other nursery rhymes are intended to help older children learn new concepts. Perhaps you even learned your ABCs through a nursery rhyme! Some rhymes help children remember the days of the week or months of the year. And some try to teach a moral, or lesson.

Not all rhymes for older children are teaching rhymes, though. Some are amusing verse stories, or stories written in rhyme. Other rhymes are tongue twisters that are fun—and a challenge—to say. And some, such as "London Bridge," are games.

Although new nursery rhymes are rarely written today, writing **parodies** of older rhymes has become quite common. In a parody, the words of a nursery rhyme are changed in a humorous way. For example, the following poem by English author Lewis Carroll is a parody of "Twinkle, Twinkle, Little Star."

Lewis Carroll

Twinkle, twinkle, little bat!
How I wonder what you're at!
Up above the world you fly,
Like a tea tray in the sky.

Some people say that imitations such as parodies are a compliment to the influence of nursery rhymes. And these rhymes certainly deserve the compliment! They have comforted, taught, amused, and tickled countless generations of children. They have also helped to encourage a love of poetry in the youngest minds. Once you have learned to listen to the lighthearted rhyme and rhythm of a nursery rhyme, it is easy to appreciate the sounds and ideas of new types of poetry.

1. Star in a nursery rhyme. Many nursery rhymes tell stories that can be made into plays. Choose one of your favorite nursery rhymes. Get together with some friends to act out the poem. For example, if you chose the rhyme "Hey Diddle Diddle," you would need people to play the cat, the cow, the dog, the dish, and the spoon. After you've practiced your play, perform it for your family or friends.

2. Parody fun. Writing a parody of a nursery rhyme can help you learn more about the rhyme scheme and rhythm of the poem. Choose a nursery rhyme and look at it carefully. Figure out its rhyme scheme. Read it out loud and listen closely to its rhythm. Now, write a parody of the nursery rhyme. Be sure to follow the same rhyme scheme and rhythm of the original poem. But make the poem as silly as you want!

Becker, Helaine. *Mother Goose Unplucked: Twisted Fairy Tales, Nutty Nursery Rhymes, and Other Wacky Takes on Childhood Favorites.* Toronto: Maple Tree Press, 2006.

Grey, Mini. *The Adventures of the Dish and the Spoon.* New York: Alfred A. Knopf, 2006.

Gustafson, Scott. *Favorite Nursery Rhymes from Mother Goose.* Shelton, Conn.: Greenwich Workshop, 2007.

Opie, Iona Archibald. *Mother Goose's Little Treasures.* Cambridge, Mass.: Candlewick Press, 2007.

GLOSSARY

nonsense—something that does not have meaning or does not make sense

orally—communicated by word of mouth, or talking

parodies—writings that copy another piece of writing in a funny way

rhyme scheme—the pattern of rhymes in a poem; a rhyme scheme shows which lines rhyme with which other lines

rhythm—the pattern of sounds or stresses in a line of poetry

stress—emphasis; words given more stress are said louder or with more force than other words

superstitions—beliefs that good or bad luck come from specific actions

syllables—complete units of sound that make up words; for example, "sit" has one syllable, and "si-lent" has two

vendors—people who sell things

BIBLIOGRAPHY

Delamar, Gloria. *Mother Goose: From Nursery to Literature*. Jefferson, N.C.: McFarland and Company, 1987.

McGraw, H. Ward, ed. *Prose and Poetry for Enjoyment*. Chicago: L. W. Singer Co., 1935.

Opie, Iona, and Peter Opie, eds. *The Oxford Dictionary of Nursery Rhymes*. Oxford: Oxford University Press, 1997.

Roberts, Chris. *Heavy Words Lightly Thrown: The Reason behind the Rhyme*. New York: Gotham Books, 2005.

Sackville-West, V. *Nursery Rhymes*. London: Dropmore Press, 1947.

INDEX

WITHDRAWN

WITHDRAWN

Community Library
PO Box 2127